MAS

Trademarks designed by
Chermayeff & Geismar

25⁰⁰

Trademarks designed by
Chermayeff & Geismar

Ivan Chermayeff
Tom Geismar
Steff Geissbuhler

Lars Müller Publishers

Published by
Lars Müller Publishers
5401 Baden/Switzerland
books@lars-muller.ch

Distributed by
Birkhäuser Publishers for Architecture,
Basel/Switzerland

ISBN 3-907078-31-4

Project editing:
Clare Jacobson

On West 57th Street in New York sits a fat, bright red, giant "9." I love it. This logo for a commercial building is probably the only trademark that not only doubles as a street number but also developed into a meeting point, a landmark. This is corporate design at its best: it serves the interests of the client and simultaneously makes the world—or at least 57th street—a better place.

Trademarks are to corporations what glasses are to wine: they will influence ever so slightly how you will perceive their content. However, at the end of the day it will be the quality of the wine that will determine your opinion. Just as you will serve a Mouton Rothschild in a crystal glass, an accomplished corporation should have a competent mark. But the most capable mark is useless if the corporation it stands for is lousy.

I think it is important that those marks are designed by "good" designers. After all, these are the jobs that get the largest exposure and thus have the biggest influence on our culture. Chermayeff & Geismar are good at it. They not only design excellent trademarks, they helped to invent this entire category. They produced an incredible diversity of ideas, styles, and forms for an incredible diversity of clients, from multinational corporations to East Village nightclubs, from enormous government projects to tiny cultural endeavors. And they were able to turn the old design adage that the finest work is always done for the smallest clients around. Some of their best work was developed for the really big ones: just think of the red "O" in Mobil (my favorite) or the peacock for NBC.

Trademarks are the one area of design where timelessness really is an issue. Nobody cares if a poster, a web site, or a magazine layout looks old fashioned next year; they get thrown out and revisited only in archives and award books. Many of the marks in this book have been utilized by their clients for decades. I find it difficult to tell which are from the eighties, which from the sixties, which from the nineties. They are that good.

Special thanks to Lars Müller,
of Lars Müller Publishers, for
his enthusiastic involvement
with this book

Making a Mark

Ivan Chermayeff
Tom Geismar
Steff Geissbuhler

This is a book of public images: a retrospective collection of trademarks designed by a single firm over forty years. The marks represent all kinds of organizations: large and small corporations, television networks, cultural institutions, social service and government agencies, banks, brands, schools, stores, hotels, and even national celebrations. They take many forms—symbols, logotypes, acronyms, and monograms—and are expressed in many styles. But each was deliberately designed to provide a distinctive, memorable, and appropriate visual expression of the organization it represents.

Chermayeff & Geismar was founded in 1960, at a time when professional practice in identity design was just taking shape. One of our starting points was the Modernist idea that design could bring the diverse visual aspects of an organization, from printed communication to architecture, together into a coherent public image. Deeper experience led us to develop processes and principles that reliably guide the creative process, and taught us to humanize Modernism's utopian ideals through humor, artistic invention, and entrepreneurial spirit.

A quick glance through the book shows a great number of bold marks, in a wide range of styles. The eclecticism is a result of a consistent, disciplined, but creatively open process that leads to a variety of solutions reflective of the radically different needs of the organizations represented. This ecumenical approach draws inspiration from all forms of conceptual and visual expression: the worlds of fine art and street art, high culture and popular culture, media and marketplace—the visible traces of all human activity. The bold forms we often favor reflect a practical reality: since trademarks must be reproducible at all sizes—from postage stamps to vehicle markings—and in all media—from print to electronic—bold forms are often most effective.

The work here is presented in roughly chronological order, though the timeline is sacrificed somewhat in order to group marks for similar organizations together. What is shown is just the tip of the iceberg. Many of the marks in this book are part of comprehensive identification programs that can only be hinted at here through accompanying illustrations. In almost every case, these programs include related color schemes, type styles, and graphic attitudes that help define a clear, visual vocabulary.

Many of the older marks in this book are still around, and still effective, partly because of a conscious effort to take a long-term view in designing them. Trademarks, by definition, must last well beyond the fashions of the moment. They must thrive with repetition. And they must survive changing markets, technology, and business practices in order to uphold a persistent and continuously relevant identity for their owners.

The pace of change continues to accelerate. As electronic media expands to become a more dominant form of visual communication, as animation becomes more widespread, and as technology makes it easier for designers to develop, test, distribute, and implement more complex imagery, trademarks and identity systems too will evolve. They will take advantage of the new technologies and the continually expanding use of colors and movement in our evolving multi-media world. But judgement, concept, skill, and experience will still be the crucial elements of successful trademark design, because the essential qualities that make a mark effective remain surprisingly constant. Now, as much as ever, we believe the process of designing trademarks continues to be grounded in a disciplined series of steps:

Listening objectively to the client's description of the problem.

Evaluating the problem in the context of current and future needs.

Defining a conceptual approach from which design development can begin.

Creating a series of design possibilities, while weeding out the merely fashionable.

Presenting the proposed design with examples of the mark in use.

Guiding effective implementation and evolution.

In listening, the designer should not just listen to the chairman's wish list. Instead, ask what, exactly, makes this organization unique. (In an age of international conglomerates with invented names, this question takes on terrific urgency.) How is it perceived by its clients, employees, vendors, and competitors? Where is the organization now, and where does it want to go in the future? What should this mark represent? Like a detective or archaeologist, the designer must listen, observe, and search for clues to the core character of the organization. Asking the right questions, of the right people, at the right time, is the key to defining appropriate performance criteria for the mark.

In evaluating, we ask questions of ourselves—and of the information we have collected. Who is the competition? What do they look like? What might be their future needs? What changes might occur to the mark through exposure? If an existing mark is being redesigned, why? (If the new CEO wants to mark his reign with a new logo, or if the board thinks a new image will save a lagging business, change may hurt more than help.)

In defining the approach, the criteria necessarily change from client to client. But such characteristics as memorability, appropriateness, legibility, and flexibility are almost always desirable. Media must also be considered, of course: a mark that will flash by on a screen has different requirements than one that will be mounted to the side of a building. Less obviously, the level of exposure the mark will receive is also pivotal—if a mark will have wide exposure, more liberties can be taken with it. The contexts in which the mark will be seen, and the audiences it will address, may demand specific symbolic meanings, visual languages, and social attitudes. Together, these considerations provide a set of restrictions and requirements that is specific to each client. They become the performance criteria that helps guide the design study, and limit the territory that needs to be explored.

In creating design possibilities, we usually produce many initial concept sketches. Often, the concepts are based on pictorial symbols, words, and letters, or a combination of the three. Combinations of seemingly disparate elements, such as a letterform and an image, or of two distinct but related images can result in a mark that is more than the sum of its parts. Through careful manipulation of content, shape, and form, a powerful new image can be formed. After a few weeks of such exploration, we start to weed out the ideas. The first to go are the merely fashionable—however appealing this year's model may be, fashion has no place in trademark design. As the saying goes, "Nothing dulls faster than the cutting edge." The next to be culled are those that do not fit the performance criteria. The designs that remain are are the most original and appropriate, and have the best potential for establishing a memorable identity.

In presenting a proposed design, we always demonstrate how it will appear in actual use. The mark, by itself, isolated on a white board, can be very deceptive. It is much more informative to show realistic mock-ups of the mark in a range of typical applications: at large sizes and small, in color and black-and-white, and in various media, from distorted faxes to sophisticated computer animations.

In guiding effective implementation, it is clear that the mark alone can never convey all the dense meanings the sponsor may desire—all it can do is make a promise. Those denser meanings can only be created over time, and most of them are created by the actions of the organization: their products, services, and relationships. From the standpoint of visual communication, though, any organization of reasonable size can be given guidelines as to the use of their trademarks and related visual systems. Color palettes, type treatments, and image selection—as well as visual attitude—can add nuance, character, and adaptability to the visual identity.

Adaptability is critical. For an identity to maintain vitality and relevance over time, its visual language must be flexible, ready to evolve in ways that cannot be predicted. The trick is to balance the need for adaptability with the need for consistency. We try to do this by providing strict guidelines for the basic identity elements, such as the trademark, signature, and, perhaps, color. But we bypass rigid formulas for all applications in favor of flexible graphic systems, which are particularly appropriate when the identity is being used in such short-lived applications as advertising, web sites, and promotional materials, where change of pace, idea, and content are essential to success.

This creative approach succeeds best when the people with whom we work know themselves, and come to the firm with clear direction. The first necessity in creating any kind of identity, whether social, political, personal, or corporate, is to know where you come from, what you stand for, and where you are headed—exactly the kinds of information we listen for in the first stage of every project.

When all is said and done, a mark is both form and substance, image and idea. To be effective, its forms must be familiar enough to be recognizable, and unusual enough to be memorable. The design must be simple enough to be read in an instant, and rich enough in detail or meaning to be interesting. It must be contemporary enough to reflect its epoch, yet not so much of its time as to appear dated before the decade is out. It must be flexible enough to evolve as society and its owner change, yet strong enough to create continuity. Finally, it must be memorable, and appropriate to the ideas and activities it represents. Trademark design challenges us to use all the magic and intelligence at our command, all our skill, knowledge, vision, and ability, in the creation of a single, clear, direct image that will embody the character and aspirations of the organizations that come to us in search of identity.

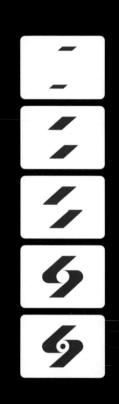

Mobil

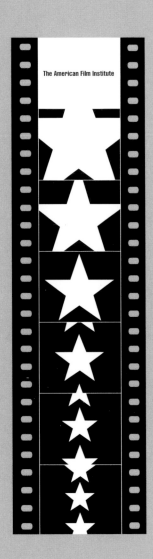

5   American Revolution
    Bicentennial Commission
    Official symbol of the
    United States bicentennial

XEROX

CRAFTON

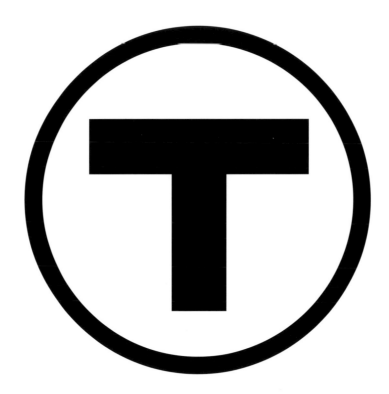

Emergence of Identity	Expressions of Identity	Crisis in Values	Future of Learning	Creativity and the Learning Process
The Right to Read	Myths of Education	Educational Hardware	Keeping Children Healthy	Making Children Healthy
Handicapped	Injured	Changing Families	Children and Parents	Family Planning Family Economics
Day Care	Children Without Prejudice	Environment	Child Development and Mass Media	Leisure Time
Rights of Children	Children in Trouble	The Child Advocate	Communicating the Law	Child Service Institutions

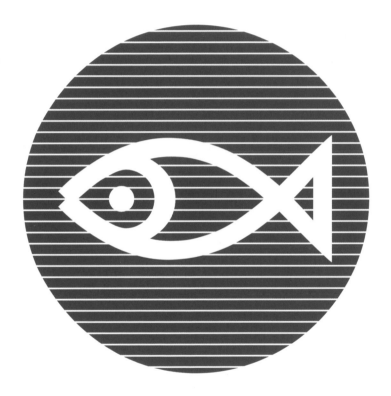

THE PORT AUTHORITY
OF NY & NJ

PERKIN-ELMER

THE ROOSEVELT

The Barclay

The Commodore

The Biltmore

OLYMPIC
TOWER

**United Banks
of Colorado, Inc.**

 **United Bank
of Aurora**

 **United Bank
of Boulder**

 **United Bank
of Denver**

 **United Bank
of Fort Collins**

 **United Bank
of Greeley**

 **United Bank
of Lakewood**

 **United Bank
of Littleton**

 **United Bank
of Pueblo**

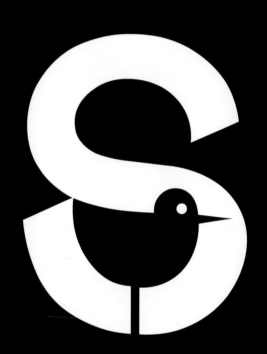

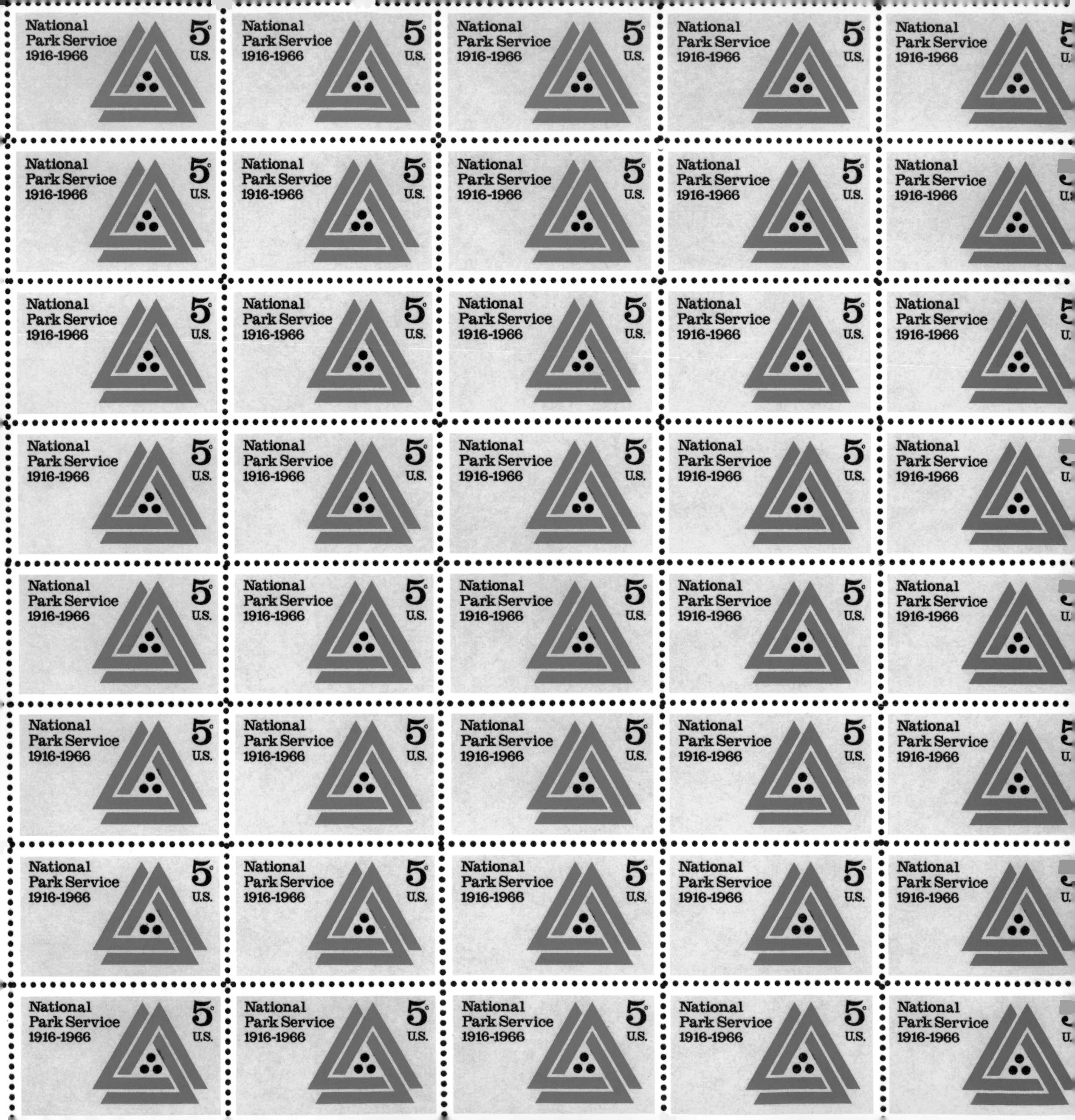
National
Park Service
1916-1966
5¢
U.S.

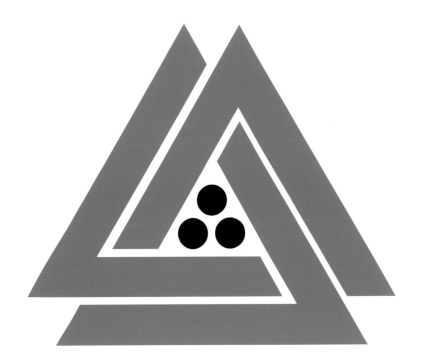

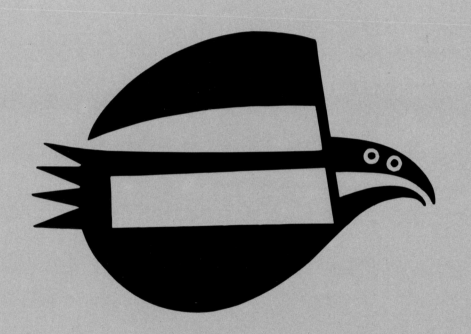

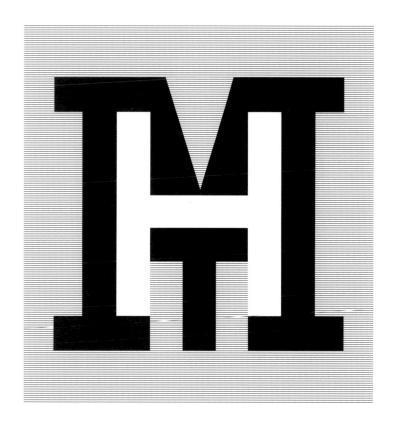

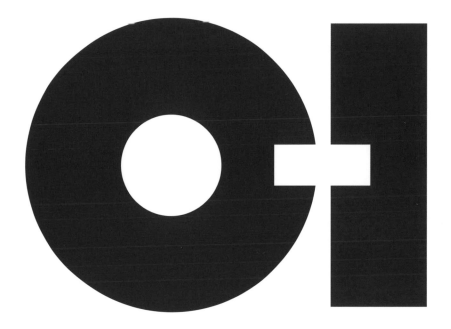

UARCO

BRENTANO'S

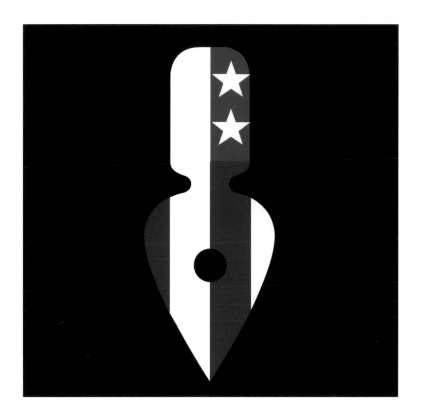

39   Torin
Air-moving equipment, wire
and strip-forming machinery

The Museum of Modern Art

The Museum of Modern Art

The Museum of Modern Art

The Hudson River Museum

47 The May Department Stores Company
Hecht's
Strawbridge's
Foley's
Robinson's-May
Filene's
Kaufmann's
Famous Barr
L.S. Ayres
The Jones Store

BEST

➤Arrow➤
from Cluett

Van Raalte
from Cluett

ATLANTIC
from Cluett

•SANFORIZED•
from Cluett

GOLD TOE
from Cluett

from Cluett

Thaibook

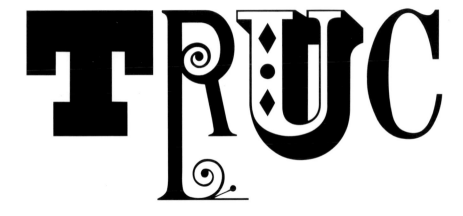

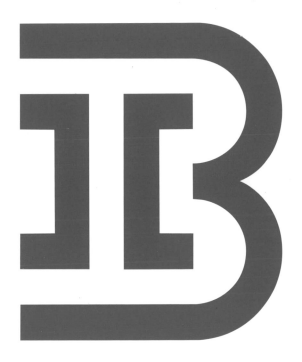

55 Ohio Center
Convention and coliseum complex
Columbus, Ohio

56 Pan American World Congress
of Architects
Washington, DC

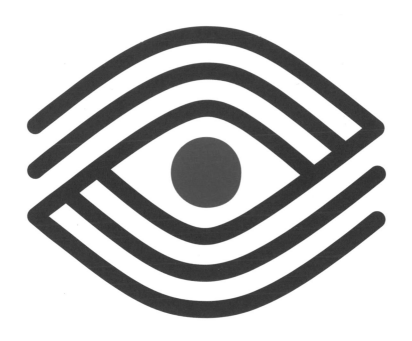

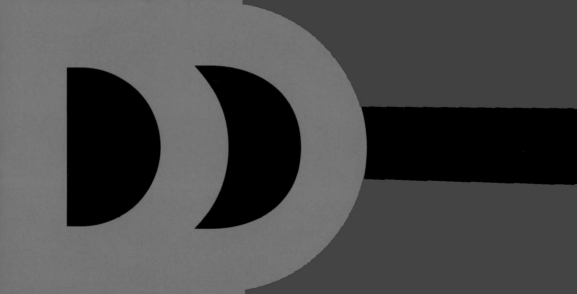

Americare

62 Americare
Product of American Republic
Insurance

63 American Republic Life
Insurance Company
Des Moines, Iowa

PICNÍQUE

Harry's

INNERPLAN

DARLING DAUGHTERS
SWEET MOTHERS DANCE
BLACKLIGHT DYNAMITE
ACROBATS ASTROLOGERS
JUGGLERS FREAKS CLOWNS
ESCAPE ARTISTS VIOLINISTS
GROK GRAPES GRASS
UPS DOWNS SIDEWAYS
AIR-CONDITIONED
IN MORE WAYS THAN ONE
THE ULTIMATE LEGAL
ENTERTAINMENT EXPERIENCE

THE ELECTRIC CIRCUS
OPENS JUNE 28, 1967
23 ST. MARK'S PLACE, N.Y.C.
EAST VILLAGE
THINK ABOUT IT.

THE ELECTRIC CIRCUS

The Way
It Was

NOVA

About
the House

WGBH TV
Boston

Leonardo

DESIGN MEDIA

National Symphony

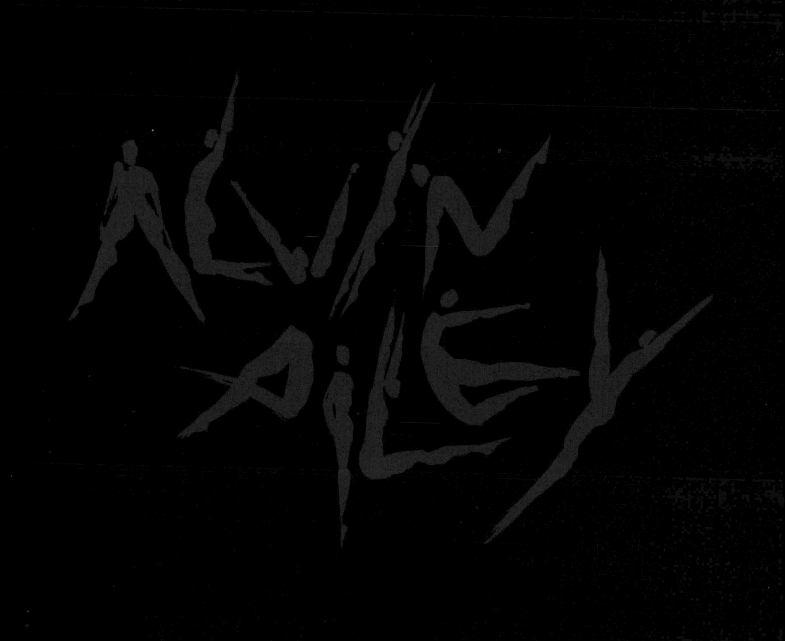

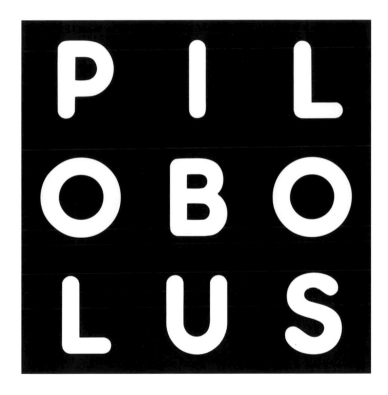

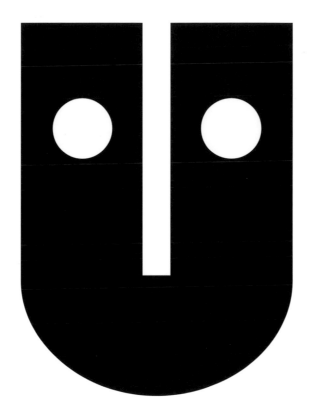

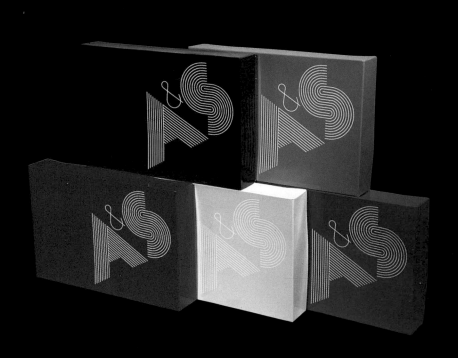

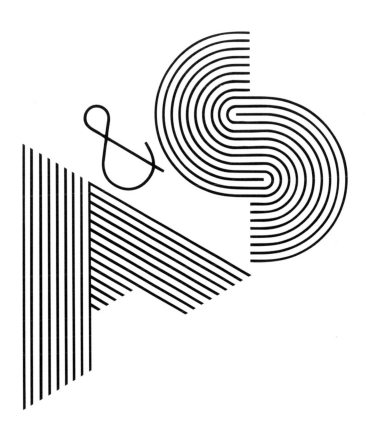

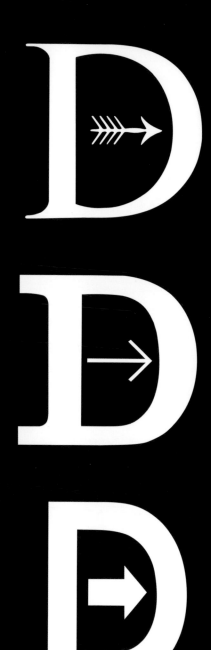

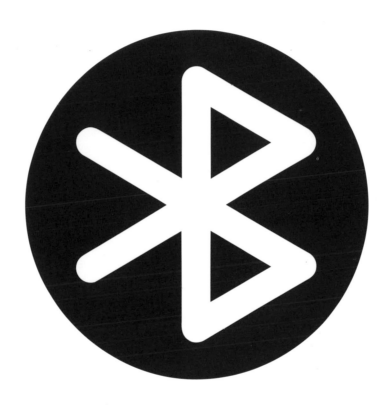

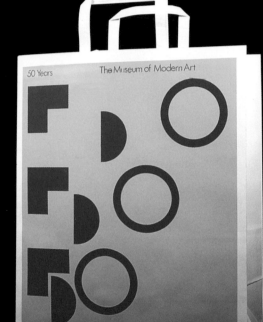

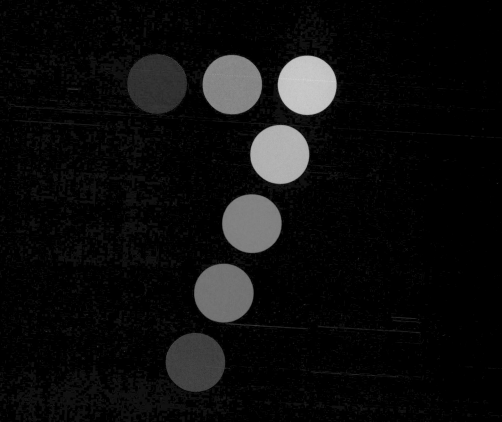

91　WNEV
Television Channel 7
Boston

92　SFX Entertainment
Promoter, producer, and venue operator
for live entertainment events

REQUEST

MIDSOUTH
MIDSOUTH

GREY

ROCKEFELLER
CENTER

ROCKEFELLER
CENTER

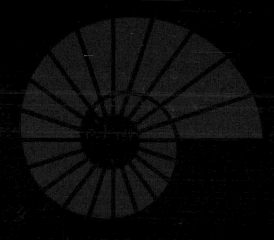

THE FIRST NEW YORK INTERNATIONAL FESTIVAL OF THE ARTS

PRECISION, INC.

PaineWebber

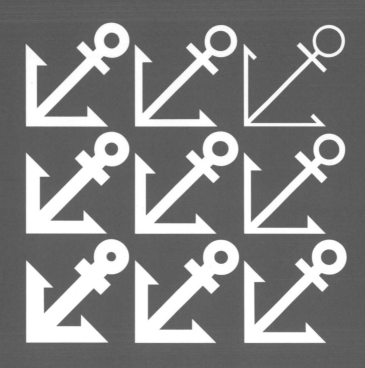

114 Anchor Engraving

115 Sailfish Point
Real estate development
Florida

116 Preservation League of New York State

117 Integrated Living Communities
National chain for assisted living

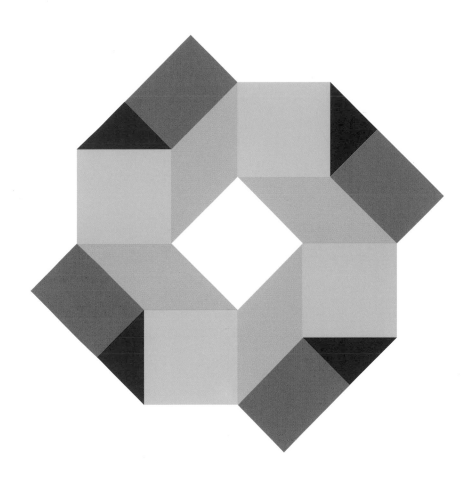

CHARLES SQUARE

(Compri)

MORGAN STANLEY

W●RLD POLICY

DIME.

The Sea Grill

GRAMAVISION

MUSEUM of ART

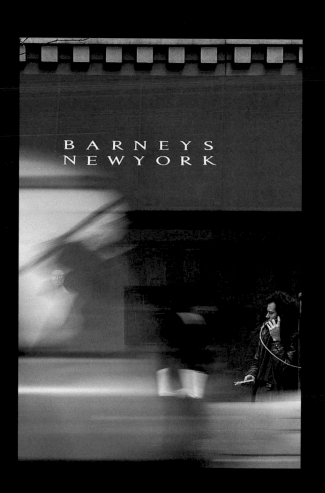

BARNEYS
NEWYORK

VIACOM

UNIVISION

"We are what we repeatedly do. Excellence, then, is not an act, but a habit." Aristotle

GEMINI

Gemini Consulting
Worldwide Leader in
Business Transformation.℠

"The world we have created today has problems which cannot be solved by thinking the way we thought when we created them."

GEMINI

Gemini Consulting
Worldwide Leader in
Business Transformation.℠

"The measure of success is not whether you have a tough problem to deal with, but whether it's the same problem you had last year."

GEMINI

Gemini Consulting
Worldwide Leader in
Business Transformation.℠

CONRAD

HOTELS

144 Conrad Hotels
International subsidiary of Hilton USA

145 Hotel Mia
Miami International Airport Hotel

HOTEL MIA

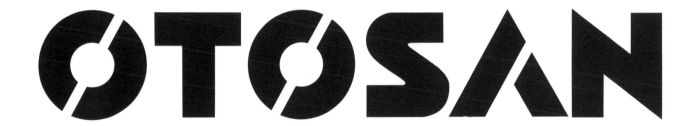

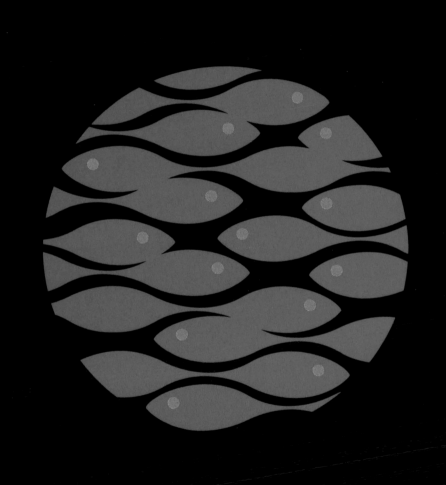

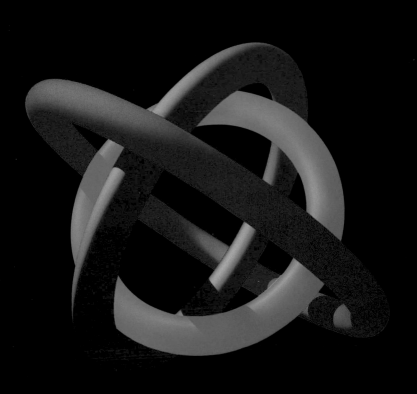

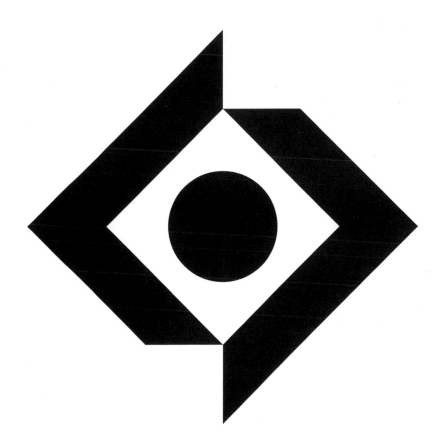

Hansol

CYCOLOR

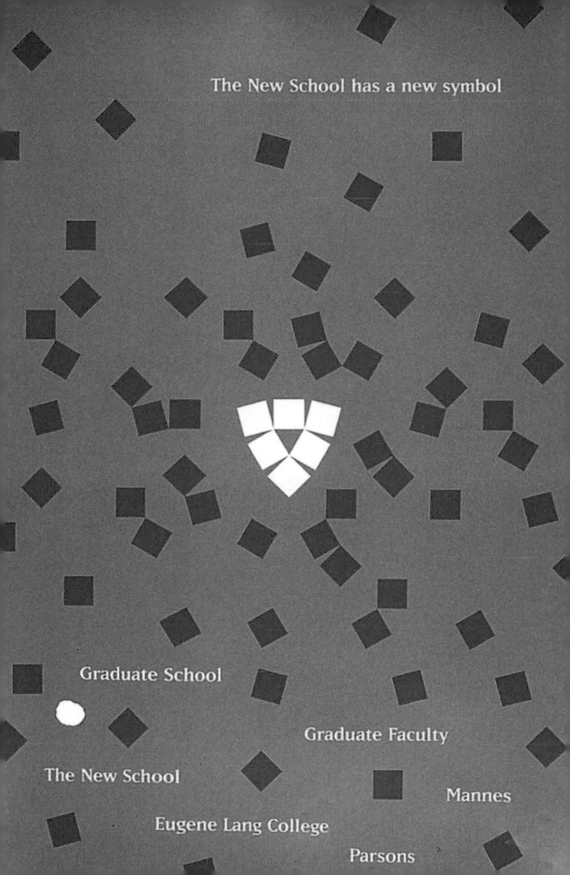

The New School has a new symbol

Graduate School

Graduate Faculty

The New School

Mannes

Eugene Lang College

Parsons

MERCK

MERCK
Human Health

MERCK
Manufacturing Division

MERCK
Research Laboratories

MERCK
AgVet Division

MERCK
Vaccine Division

MERCK
Consumer Healthcare Group

MERCK
Specialty Chemicals Group

MSD

161 Merck
Worldwide research-intensive pharmaceutical,
health, and agricultural and veterinarian products

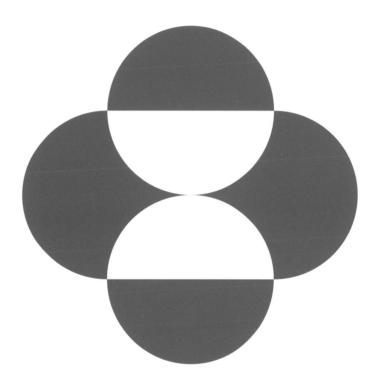

U
M
B
R
E
L
L
A

FACTSET

Mount
Sinai

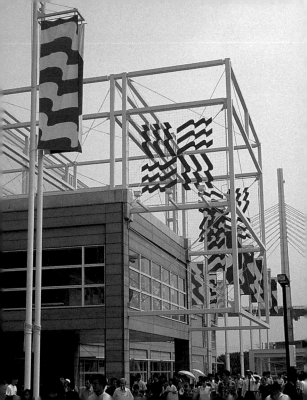

174 The New Victory Theater
Broadway theater for children
New York

175 New 42nd Street Inc.
Organization for the revitalization
of the 42nd Street theaters
New York

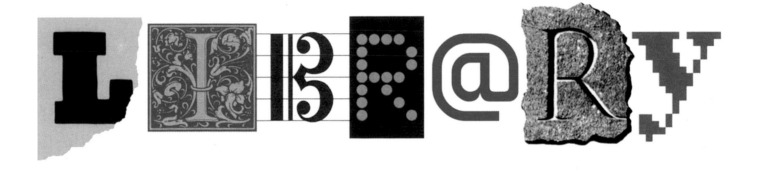

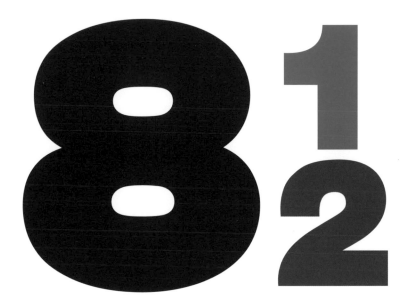

Insignia

185   Heritage Trails
        Walking tours of historic sites
        Lower Manhattan

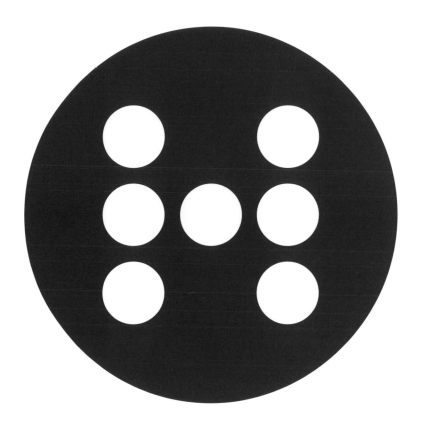

187   Old Chatham Sheepherding Company
Sheep's milk products
Old Chatham, New York

188 Sunshine Amalgamated
Movie theater company
New York

189 Rio Algom
International mining company

 Smithsonian
Anacostia Museum

 Smithsonian
Archives of American Art

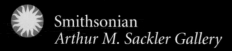 Smithsonian
Arthur M. Sackler Gallery

 Smithsonian
Cooper-Hewitt, National Design Museum

 Smithsonian
Freer Gallery of Art

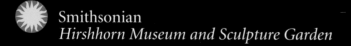 Smithsonian
Hirshhorn Museum and Sculpture Garden

 Smithsonian
National Air and Space Museum

 Smithsonian
National Museum of African Art

 Smithsonian
National Museum of American Art

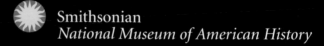 Smithsonian
National Museum of American History

Smithsonian
National Museum of the American Indian

Smithsonian
National Museum of Natural History

Smithsonian
National Portrait Gallery

Smithsonian
National Postal Museum

Smithsonian
National Zoological Park

193   Eli's Manhattan
Gourmet food stores
New York

ibid.

194 Ibid
Stock photo company
Chicago

195 Powered by Cummins' Kids
Daycare center
Columbus, Indiana

O'K

I·N·F·I·N·E·E·R

PRISMA

kidpower

With gratitude to all the people and organizations who have given us the opportunity to express their identity through design.

Among the leaders in design for over forty years, Chermayeff & Geismar Inc. (C&G) maintains its position by fostering the philosophy that has always guided the firm's success. Quite simply, effective design is a process that must lead from an understanding of a problem to an image that is succinct, memorable, long-lasting, and appropriate to the entity it represents. This process assures clients of a well-considered visual interpretation rather than a design that says more about the design firm than about the client.

The firm's partners, Ivan Chermayeff, Tom Geismar, and Steff Geissbuhler, have achieved substantial recognition for their individualized approach to solving clients' problems over a wide range of design disciplines. Along with major identification programs, the work also encompasses all aspects of graphic design, environmental graphics, interactive media, and the development of major thematic and historical exhibitions.

The firm has received numerous design awards for its clients from all the major professional organizations, and its work has been exhibited throughout the world.